Animals of the Night

AARDVARKS AFTER DARK

Heather M. Moore Niver

Enslow Publishing
101 W. 23rd Street
Suite 240
New York, NY 10011
USA

enslow.com

Words to Know

burrow—An animal's home or protection that is often a hole in the ground or a tunnel.

gland—An organ that makes and releases substances into the body or gets rid of substances.

habitat—The place in which an animal lives.

mammals—Animals that have a backbone and hair, usually give birth to live babies, and produce milk to feed their young.

nocturnal—Mostly active at night.

predators—Animals that kill and eat other animals to stay alive.

saliva—A liquid in the mouth that helps with chewing and swallowing.

savannah—A habitat area with lots of grass but not very many trees.

termite—A winged, light-colored insect that eats wood.

Contents

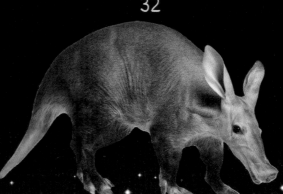

Leaving Home

After a long hot day, the aardvark stretches. It's getting dark and the **nocturnal** aardvark is hungry. It's ready to head out to hunt. Pausing at its **burrow** entry, it looks out for enemies. The coast is clear. The aardvark runs out and begins to jump around. It looks around again for danger. It jumps around again. Satisfied that all is safe, the aardvark wanders off in search of ants and **termites**.

The aardvark uses its long, flexible nose to sniff out insects. When it finds a nest, it uses long claws to dig down to its next meal.

An aardvark checks for danger before leaving its den for a meal. They eat more ants than termites.

In the Sand Where the Digging Is Easy

An aardvark is more than just a funny-looking animal with a funny-looking name. This curious critter is a **mammal** that lives in southern Africa south of the Sahara Desert. But they don't just live in the hot sandy desert. Aardvarks live in **habitats** like rain forests and **savannahs**, too. They just need to get their favorite food (termites), water to drink, and soft, sandy soil to dig.

Aardvarks are great diggers. They dig to get to those tasty termites. But if the ground is too tough, they'll move to a new area.

FUN FACT!

The word "aardvark" means "earth pig" in a local South African language. Some people also call them "ant bear."

Aardvarks can live happily as long as there is water, soft sand for digging and (of course) a good supply of their favorite food: termites!

The Awkward Aardvark

Aardvarks are odd beasts. They do look a bit like pigs, with a long body and snout. But they have long ears like a rabbit or a donkey. And their tail looks like that of a kangaroo!

The aardvark's body is covered with coarse hair. It may be yellow-gray in color. The aardvark doesn't have much hair. Its face and the tip of its tail are often a shade of white. The rest of its skin ranges from a light dull yellow to pink.

FUN FACT!

Sometimes the aardvark's skin gets stained a darker gray or dark brown-red by the dirt in which it digs.

Believe it or not, aardvarks are related to elephants and manatees!

The aardvark is a heavy animal. It weighs between 110 and 180 pounds (50 to 82 kilograms). Its head and body are around 43 to 53 inches (109 to135 centimeters). The tail adds another 21 to 26 inches (53 to 66 cm).

An aardvark has short legs, but they are strong. Their claws are great tools for digging. Those claws are sharp and shaped like shovels. It has four claws on each of its front feet and five on each of its back feet.

The aardvark's short legs are very strong and great for digging for termites and ants.

Underground Dining

Aardvarks like a meal of ants and termites. They are well-shaped to catch these underground treats. Termites build and live in nests that rise a little bit out of the ground. They live in big groups. Aardvarks know to look for these mounds. There will be lots to eat underneath!

After the sun goes down, it's time to eat. Aardvarks use their claws to break through the mound. They have a long, sticky tongue. It's a bit like a worm. That tongue can reach almost 1 foot (30 cm)!

FUN FACT!

Aardvarks can close their noses so no dust or insects get in there. Their skin is thick, so insect bites don't bother them one bit.

An aardvark's tongue is long and sticky. It is perfect for catching

After the aardvark breaks the mound, the insects are trapped. They get stuck on the aardvark's tongue. Its tongue is covered with sticky **saliva**. Sometimes there are termites or ants the aardvark can't reach with its tongue. In that case, the aardvark knows to use its nose. It pushes its nose against the hole in the mound and sucks up its meal.

Aardvarks never chew their food. They swallow the ants and termites whole! They have a special part of their stomach that grinds them up. An aardvark might eat as many as 50,000 insects in one night. Yum!

Aardvarks stick their snout into the ground to suck up more insects to eat.

Aardvarks in Action

A hungry aardvark might travel for miles in one night to seek out ants and termites. They walk in a zig-zag pattern. They explore a path that is about 100 feet (30 meters) wide. Their flexible nose helps them sniff out their next meal. Aardvarks have a keen sense of smell.

Their vision is terrible during the day, but they can see at night. Even at night they can't see colors, though.

FUN FACT!

Aardvarks don't move very fast. They walk slowly on their claws. Their long tail drags behind and leaves a mark in the ground.

The claws of an aardvark make walking a little clumsy, but they are useful when it comes time to dig for dinner.

Aardvarks are incredible diggers. In fact, you could probably argue that they are better diggers than humans! They can dig through tough termite mounds, for example. A human needs a sharp, pointy axe to break through. An aardvark just needs its claws and muscles. Aardvarks are also superfast diggers. They can dig a hole faster than several humans with shovels.

Digging comes in handy when they need to escape danger, too. They can dig fast and deep in no time at all.

Aardvarks are expert diggers. They are fast and strong when they dig through a termite mound.

Aardvarks at Home

During the day, an aardvark curls up in a comfy burrow underground. Sometimes they choose a temporary home that is not very deep. Other times they dig a deep, complicated burrow. It can be as deep as 19 feet (6 m) underground. It might have lots of tunnels. Some burrows have eight entries. The entrances might be mostly filled up. Aardvarks leave a small hole for air. During the day, the aardvark curls up in a ball tight against an entry. Deeper burrows are used when it's time for the aardvark to give birth.

FUN FACT!

Sometimes aardvarks like a nice nap in the sun. They will come out of their dens when it is cold. The sun warms them up.

The aardvark's super digging skills also help it make its own burrow.

Adorable Aardvark Babies

Aardvarks live on their own most of the time. A mother aardvark usually gives birth to one baby at a time. Sometimes she has two.

Baby aardvarks are born without a single bit of hair. Their eyes are open when they are born. For the first two months, they drink milk from their mother. They remain in the burrow all this time. After that, it's time to eat insects. They follow their mother and learn how to dig and hunt for insects.

An aardvark usually gives birth to just one baby each year.

Baby aardvarks stay with their mothers for about six months. Then it's time to go off on their own. At this point they can hunt for their own food. Young aardvarks can also dig their own burrows. They can have babies of their own after age two. Most aardvarks live to be about eighteen years old in the wild. In more protected areas like zoos they can live up to about twenty-four years old.

FUN FACT!

Scientists have a tough time figuring out how many aardvarks there are. Aardvarks move around a lot. They change dens often. And of course they are mainly active at night.

Aardvark babies are born with claws.

Aardvark Talk

The aardvark is a loner, so maybe that's why it doesn't talk all that much. The only sounds it is known to make is a grunt. When it is scared it might make a bleating sound.

To communicate with other aardvarks, scientists think they use scent. Aardvarks have **glands** on their elbows and hips. They might mark areas in the soil with these glands. When two aardvarks meet, they give one another a sniff. They especially smell around the other aardvark's tail, where there may be more scent glands. Then they go off on their own again.

Aardvarks don't talk much, but they leave scent marks by marking
the soil using glands on their elbows.

Aardvark Predators

Humans sometimes hunt aardvarks. Some think their teeth have the ability to keep people from getting sick. Other parts of their bodies might be used, too. Sometimes they are hunted for their meat. **Predators** such as lions, hyenas, and leopards are always a worry for aardvarks.

Another concern for aardvarks is keeping their natural habitat. Humans take up more and more space. They build more buildings, for example. This means they are taking up the places where wild animals like aardvarks need to live.

Aside from digging, an aardvark's claws are also used to protect itself.

Stay Safe Around Aardvarks

Aardvarks are known for being shy. Some scientists have trouble seeing them in the wild! You would be very lucky to see one.

Most people who see aardvarks catch them busy digging. The aardvark runs away as soon as it sees the human. If they are near their burrow, they will hide in there. They might exit from another entry the human can't see. But if attacked, an aardvark has claws and strong legs. It will gash and kick.

It's not even easy to see aardvarks at zoos! Some zoos have special exhibits to show nocturnal creatures.

Elan, Gidon C

91832

Thursday, January 7, 2021

31183182788361   Aardvarks after dark

Learn More

Books

Borgert-Spaniol, Megan. *Aardvarks*. Minneapolis: Bellwether Media, 2014.

Gibbs, Maddie. *Aardvarks*. New York: PowerKids Press, 2011.

Gregory, Josh. *Aardvarks*. New York: Children's Press, 2015.

Websites

National Geographic: Aardvark

animals.nationalgeographic.com/animals/mammals/
  aardvark/
  Check out photos, facts, maps, and more!

Wildscreen Arkive: Aardvark

www.arkive.org/aardvark/orycteropus-afer/
  This site features photos and facts about aardvarks.

Index

Published in 2017 by Enslow Publishing, LLC.
101 W. 23rd Street, Suite 240, New York, NY 10011

Copyright © 2017 by Enslow Publishing, LLC.

Library of Congress Cataloging-in-Publication Data

Names: Niver, Heather Moore, author.

Title: Aardvarks after dark / Heather M. Moore Niver.

Description: New York, NY : Enslow Publishing, 2017. | Series: Animals of the night | Includes bibliographical references and index.

Identifiers: LCCN 2015048672| ISBN 9780766077096 (library bound) | ISBN 9780766077386 (pbk.) | ISBN 9780766076846 (6-pack)

Subjects: LCSH: Aardvark—Behavior—Juvenile literature. | Aardvark—Juvenile literature.

Classification: LCC QL737.T8 N58 2017 | DDC 599.3/1—dc23

LC record available at http://lccn.loc.gov/2015048672

Printed in the United States of America

To Our Readers: We have done our best to make sure all website addresses in this book were active and appropriate when we went to press. However, the author and the publisher have no control over and assume no liability for the material available on those websites or on any websites they may link to. Any comments or suggestions can be sent by e-mail to customerservice@enslow.com.

Photo Credits: Throughout book, narvikk/E+/Getty Images (starry background), kimberrywood/Digital Vision Vectors/Getty Images (green moon dingbat); cover, p. 1 Christian Colista.Shutterstock.com, samxmed/E+/Getty Images (moon); p. 3 Eric Isselee/Shutterstock.com; p. 5 © imageBROKER/Alamy Stock Photo; p. 7 © age fotostock/Alamy Stock Photo; p. 9 © National Geographic Creative/Alamy Stock Photo; p. 11 © Ardea/Labat, Ferrero/Animals Animals; p. 13 © Josef Vostarek/CTK Photobank/agefotostock; p. 15 © Nigel Dennis/age fotostock; pp. 17, 29 Eric Isselee/Shutterstock.com; p. 19 © Abpl/Lamberti, Stephanie/Animals Animals; p. 21 © Abpl Image Library/Animals Animals; p. 23 © WENN Ltd/Alamy Stock Photo; p. 25 © iStock.com/Robert Kovacs; p. 27 © A & J Visage/Alamy Stock Photo.